Devotion to Saint Dominic

Étienne Vayssière, O.P.

Devotion to

Saint Dominic

Translated by

George G. Christian, O.P.

2014

DNS Publication

**Devotion to Saint Dominic
by Marie-Étienne Vayssière, O.P.**

Translated by George G. Christian, O.P.

La dévotion à saint Dominique was originally published in French by Les Éditions du Cerf in *La Vie spirituelle*, n° 663, January-February 1985, p. 107-123.

IMPRIMI POTEST
Frère Gilbert Narcisse, O.P.
Prieur Provincial
Toulouse 21 July 2013

IMPRIMI POTEST
Very Rev. Brian M. Mulcahy, O.P.
Prior Provincial
New York 10 February 2014

DNS PUBLICATIONS
Dominican Nuns of Summit
543 Springfield Avenue
Summit, New Jersey 07901
www.nunsopsummit.org

ISBN: 0615966950
ISBN-13: 978-0615966953

Printed in the United States of America

Cover painting: High Altar of the Dominican Church of Frankfurt
by Hans Holbein the Elder
Cover Photo Copyright ©2013 Heidemarie Niemann, Mainz, Germany
Used by permission

CONTENTS

Devotion to Saint Dominic

FOREWORD

No one will ever extol too much the importance of authentic devotion to saints in the Catholic faith. This is neither a contamination of the faith arising from pagan polytheism nor an arbitrary outpouring of popular religion. Rather, it bears witness to an uncontaminated understanding of the mysterious generosity of God. In fact, unlike the powerful rulers of this world, God does not manifest His grandeur by creating a clear space around Himself, nor by monopolizing any genuine action. Quite the contrary, the glory of God lies in generously associating creatures to his action of salvation. St. Thomas Aquinas explains that, even though God has no need of creatures to realize his projects, He freely associates them to His action "by reason of His boundless goodness, in virtue of which He wished to grant to creatures a

1

resemblance to Himself, not only as regards existence but also as regards the reality of being the cause of others." (*Contra Gentiles*, III:70)

Clearly, there are actions that can belong to God alone; we firmly confess that Jesus Christ, and Jesus Christ alone is our Savior. But all those who are saved by Jesus Christ, who are integrated into his body, immediately become instruments of salvation for their brothers. In proportion to their union with Christ, they collaborate in the salvation of the world by their witness, by their prayer, by their sharing in the Passion of Christ.

It is a fact of life that God gives us as rain the water that flows down from the heights. It penetrates the earth and travels through several mineral layers before it emerges as a spring. Now, from every layer it passes, the water carries away some individual quality that gives the spring its taste and its singular characteristics. In like manner, the life that God communicates to us finds its source in the Holy Trinity. From there, it passes through the pierced heart of Christ, then through the Church, the Spouse of Christ, which lives by his life and communicates it to his children. This is why the life of grace is Christocentric and ecclesial.

Furthermore, in the Church, certain saints received a charism to live and to cause others to live a particular aspect of the unique and multifaceted grace of Christ. This is the case with the founders of religious families. In St. Francis of Assisi and his children, there shine and are displayed the poverty and the humility of Jesus; in St. Camillus of Lellis, his love for the sick; in Mother Teresa, her compassion.

According to Vatican II (*Perfectae caritatis*, N° 2), the vitality of religious families therefore implies "the constant return to the sources of all Christian life as well as to the original inspiration of the institutes. For this reason, the spirit of the founders and their specific goals as well as salutary traditions must be highlighted and faithfully maintained—the totality constituting the patrimony of each institute." But, as early as 1935, in a circular letter in which the *Éditions du Cerf* [publishing house] undertook the fortunate initiative of proposing to a public more extensive than its initial clientele, Father Étienne Vayssière, OP, at the time provincial of Toulouse, who was inviting his religious to rediscover what he called the *patriarchal gift* of St. Dominic. To know St. Dominic better, to fill oneself with his spirit, to develop a filial confidence in his intercession, this is the genuine devotion to St. Dominic he recommended—he whom, we are told [by Marie-Joseph Nicolas], enjoyed "the blessing of a filial union with St. Dominic." According to the fitting motto of Blessed Hyacinthe-Marie Cormier, Father Vayssière wished "to restore everything in St. Dominic."

But the very personal manner by which Fr. Vayssière was led by providential circumstances to live the Dominican way of life, conferred on his portrait of St. Dominic an original touch. The *hermit* of *Sainte-Baume*, the great contemplative that Fr. Vayssière was, could only emphasize how much the ideal of the Order of Friars Preachers, of which Dominic is the shining example, does not reside in a judicious balance between diverse juxtaposed elements (prayer, study, common life, and preaching), but finds its unity in a personal union with God, *the soul of all apostolate*. In a reflection of St. Dominic and in the very imitation of God, the apostle, according to the heart of Fr. Vayssière, is the man who *gives himself completely without ever going outside of himself.*

Friar Serge-Thomas Bonino, OP

THE FOUNDATIONS

The seventh centennial of the canonization of St. Dominic nears its end; in the crown of glory with which it envelops the patriarch of the Preachers, let our hearts rejoice. Since the celebrations of Toulouse and of Prouille, produced with such enthusiasm last July, the solemnities of the Church, the voices of the highest authorities repeated their admiration, the piety of the faithful showed itself in agreement and enthusiastic. It was a magnificent symphony of praise, and for the sons of St. Dominic, a time of pride and joy.

Throughout the centuries, that joy and that pride joined the enthusiasm that uplifted the entire

Order, when, for the first time, on 3 July 1234, the Apostolic See, through the voice of Gregory IX, proclaimed to the Catholic world the holiness of Dominic. Upon this summit of all human and divine glory, what delight to see the holy patriarch arise and shine!

As if in anticipation, everything prepared for this glorification. "I no longer doubt the holiness of St. Dominic," said Pope Gregory IX, who had known him well, "any more than I doubt the sanctity of the apostles Peter and Paul."

It awakened, in a manner of speaking, with the last beat of his heart. In fact, as reported by contemporary chronicles, his soul had barely left his body that, by a mysterious prodigy, the sorrow felt by his children suddenly changed into a fully supernatural joy. In the presence of the inanimate remains, they no longer saw their father overcome by death; they simply dwelt on his glory, in an unspeakable certitude felt deep in their hearts. A hymn of triumph followed their lamentations; an inexpressible joy, a joy of heaven, marvelously filled them.

This was the first ray of a glory that was subsequently to increase without respite.

In spite of the excessive wariness of his children, the tomb of St. Dominic began to attract crowds—unceasing miracles manifesting on earth his glory in heaven.

On the day of the reburial of his remains, an indescribable fragrance was released from, his open casket: a telling sign of the grace of holiness, which, to the astonishment of his contemporaries, never ceased to express itself throughout the centuries.

Even today, the seventh centenary caused it to shine again in an even brighter light. Following the example of our brothers of the 13th century, who had answered the appeal of Blessed Jordan to venerate and kiss the sacred remains of Dominic— and preserved on their lips, for a long time, the unspeakable perfume of that kiss—let us, in turn, approach the sacred patriarch in a filial tenderness, dwelling on a remembrance of him with lively joy;

let us plunge more deeply into his thought, his spirit, and his virtues. In a word, let us, in that filial contact, regenerate our religious and Dominican life.

One of the principal obligations of our responsibility consists in frequently reminding the brethren of the duties of their calling, along with the ideal of holiness that should motivate all their efforts. Precisely in this lies the important lesson of this centenary celebration. What it proposes to us, in St. Dominic, is less his prestige as founder and the fruitfulness of his apostolate, but rather his outstanding holiness. What it frequently repeats to us are the exalted words of the Holy Books: *Aspice et fac secundum exemplar quod tibi ostensum est in monte.* ["See that you make them according to the pattern for them, which is being shown you on the mountain."] (*Ex* 25:40)

In the presence of the soul of St. Dominic, a genuine mountain of sanctity, let us pause, open our eyes, and look at our father on those sacred heights wherein the Church placed him seven centuries ago, and where in a maternal gesture even today invites us to dwell upon him. Take a look, the better to understand and imitate him; in that glance of love and in that generosity of heart really lie the benefits and the resolutions of this centenary.

Studied in the truth of history, no description of a saint appears more attractive and sympathetic than that of Dominic. It is true that the hatred of enemies of the Church worked at defacing that picture; popular imagination, misled by incessant lies, often saw—and still today sees—the gentle patriarch of the preachers only through the instruments of torture and the flames of the stake. But it needs to be said that the truth is completely opposite. In the far-off 13th century, no one among his contemporaries showed a more appealing friendliness except this poor man of Christ, this humble and untiring missionary of Truth, traveling on foot, toting a shoulder bag, singing hymns to the Virgin, deploring the fate of sinners, kneeling down at the entrance of cities, and with tears asking the Lord not to chastize them for their sins: a living image of the Savior of the world, gentle and humble

11

of heart, passing in the midst of men while doing good.

THE NATURAL TRAITS OF OUR BLESSED FATHER

We are familiar with the charming portrait of St. Dominic traced by Sister Cecilia:

> He was average in height, well-proportioned; his body slender and nimble, his features attractive, his complexion ruddy, his hair and beard of rather vivid blond. From his forehead, between the eyebrows, there radiated a brightness that attracted respect and love. He was always joyful, pleasant, except when he was moved by some affliction of the neighbor. He had long and attractive hands, a voice noble and deep. He wore the complete religious crown, flecked with only a few white hairs. The hands of the Creator himself had fashioned this delicate body and enriched it with His grace, so that he would be for the Holy Spirit a sanctuary worthy of His gifts and of His activities.

The portrait that Blessed Jordan paints of the Blessed Father is no less attractive.

There was in him such purity of life, such a significant movement of divine fervor, such an impetuous springing towards God, that he was truly a vessel of honor and of blessing. Nothing ever troubled the equanimity of his soul, except his compassion for the misfortunes of the neighbors. The beauty and joy of his demeanor conveyed his interior serenity, such that the slightest movement of anger could never obscure; his goodness won all hearts; at the first glance of him, one felt irresistibly drawn to him; he received everyone in the depth of his charity; in loving everyone, he was loved by everyone; he gave his nights to God and his days to his neighbor. Nothing seemed more natural to him than to rejoice with those who were rejoicing, and to weep with those who were weeping. In his conduct there was never the shadow of disguise; nothing equaled the simplicity of his heart; who will ever attain the virtue of that man? We can indeed admire him, but to be able to do what he could, to imitate what he did, these are characteristics of a singular grace that God grants only to those whom He wishes to raise to the heights of sanctity.

THE HUMAN GLORY OF ST. DOMINIC

Accordingly, should we be surprised by the irresistible attraction exercised in his lifetime by St. Dominic? And is this not still today, the secret of his elevation, through the course of centuries, even up to our time? Equal to that celestial perfume which, on the occasion of the translation of his relics, elated its witnesses with unspeakable delight, the odor of his sanctity and the gentleness of his benefits never ceased, throughout the ages, to attract souls and to win them over. In the diversity of its voices, History is there to remind us: voices of Popes and of the great of this earth; voices of the lowly and the humble, voices of the people, the voice of poetry, that of the arts, of eloquence, the voice of everything here below that can vibrate and sing—all of them are united to honor Dominic and to make us see in him one of the most significant messengers of divine love to the earth, one of the most venerated patriarchs in whom the Church takes pride.

But, dare I say it, this human glory, this admiration and these congenial feelings, whatever high spirits they evoke in the hearts of his children, could not necessarily be the genuine basis for their devotion as well as the deep source of their love and of their confidence. The glory of St. Dominic has a higher origin and must be based on a more solid foundation. The genuine glory of saints appears especially in the veneration in which the Church honors them, and this admiration is measured by the glow of the divine life in their heart and by the supernatural mission entrusted to them.

Our destiny in St. Dominic

In the formation and the development of the mystical body of Christ, divine goodness by itself, is, without a doubt, infinitely sufficient; it has no need of external assistance to attain its goals. And yet, out of love for the creature and to increase he latter's glory and happiness, this divine goodness is often pleased to call for the creature's cooperation, and to associate it, as a secondary cause, to its infinite activity. Thus, says St. Thomas, the angels of the superior hierarchies enlighten the angels of the lower hierarchies. The same law operates in the world of grace and of glory. From the heart of Christ, divine home wherein it resides in its fullness, grace descends and spreads to the saints according to the measure of the gifts allotted to them. Here indeed is the point of departure for the devotion that we owe to St. Dominic.

HE IS OUR FATHER

What is Dominic's relation to our faith? He is our father. God has associated him with the ineffable mystery of His paternity. As the principle of all things, eternal love has arranged everything with infinite wisdom, has willed, chosen, and destined us in St. Dominic. It has made us Dominic's children, has connected us to him by an ineffable and vital bond. It has willed, that, like Abraham, Dominic would be the father of innumerable generations; it gave Dominic the gifts given to patriarchs.

And note well that Dominic's paternity is not simply a title of honor: it is accompanied by the grace appropriate to his important mission. In the same way that, God has given to His Christ *[Anointed One]* a full and principal grace, which, from His heart, He pours over the entire mystical Body, so too, He gave to St. Dominic, as well as to the diverse patriarchs of the religious life, that fullness of grace which was to nourish their descendants, a

17

fullness received from Christ, and which, by their agency, was to overflow into the souls of their children.

As our mediator, he interceded for us

Yet another privilege! As Christ, in the world of the elect, is the mediator for redemption and for life, just so Dominic, dependent on Him always, is for his religious family the agent for intercession. Up above, in the presence of God, he represents his children, carrying them in the tenderness of his arms, incessantly offering them to infinite mercy, to the channel of life that feeds them, to the wisdom that leads and directs them, a helpful influence in their favor, a tenderness that presses them to his chest, where it resonates like a distant echo—no doubt faint but nonetheless real—of the magnificent and eternal word: "You are my son, today I have begotten you." [Ps 2:7b] This is what Dominic is, this is what we are: he is our father, and we are his offspring. An indescribable truth! And in

18

this certainty, what dynamic and radiant light on the bonds that ought to tie us to him; how powerful and intimate they appear to us!

Moreover, this light is made even more brilliant when, after having considered in its foundation the mystery of our destiny, we study its results in the future, at the final end of the centuries, at that ultimate hour when time will have completed its course and the Son hands over all royalty to His Father.

OUR GLORIFICATION IN ST. DOMINIC

Sons of St. Dominic, what will be our place in the magnificence of the saints? In God, no doubt, in Christ who will be our all in everything. In Mary, always Mother, above, as she was here on earth. And, I do not hesitate to add, in St. Dominic, in the very heart of the glorious patriarch. In fact, the gifts of God are given without regret. The laws He has established develop in a harmony and a fidelity guaranteed by His infinite wisdom. Our glory, above, will be the crowning of that grace in which we were predestined and brought into being. Generated in St. Dominic, we will be glorified in St. Dominic. From all eternity, the Dominican family was willed and organized by God for a determined purpose in the midst of the very large family of Christ. In time, after having fulfilled its providential role, this family will find itself, in heaven above, in the integrity of its original predestination, which is to say, in St. Dominic, enlivened by his grace as patriarch, transformed in the flood of his glory, sheltered in the very heart wherein God placed its origins, and where, after having drawn from his life, in due time it would enjoy eternal rest. In him and with him, moreover, it will sing unending praise. During the days of his mortal life, the ancient chronicles tell us, at the hours of psalms and of prayer, the voice of St. Dominic would rise in the middle of choir, energetic, enthusiastic, in order to lead and support the brothers: *Viriliter fratres*, ["Act like men, brothers!"] he loved to repeat. On that day of unending praise, in the flurry of eternal and exalted psalmody, is it not appropriate for our devotion and our faith to think again about Dominic in the fire of his voice, in the rhythm of his heart and of his actions, leading his children to the embrace of eternal love?

OUR VOCATION AND OUR LIFE IN ST. DOMINIC

This is to be our eternity: in Dominic and with Dominic always. You get a glimpse of what comes next: these visions of eternity, do they not place in a definite and victorious light our life in time? Is glory anything else but grace in full bloom and raised to its highest power? The intimacy of our union with St. Dominic, prepared for by our destiny and so animated in the eternal centuries, does it not tell us better than any reasoning how deeply it must be rooted in time and how strongly the link of devotion and of love, forged by God Himself to attach us firmly and endlessly to our blessed father, needs to be maintained?

This duty appears no less pressing from a new consideration that we ought not overlook: indeed, we should not forget that our Dominican vocation was completed and fulfilled by St. Dominic at the price of very hard penances.

In fact, when, in the course of his apostolic wanderings, Dominic, alone and saddened at the sight of heresy triumphant, traveled the plains of Languedoc; when, mocked contradicted, persecuted, he walked while crying to heaven the mournful cry of his soul as apostle: "Lord, what will become of sinners?"; when, on his long trips, allowing his companions to walk ahead of him, he held heart to heart conversations with his beloved Savior; or else, with his powerful voice he fed the echoes of the plains with strophes of *Ave maris Stella*, or of *Veni Creator*, what was he asking of the Holy Spirit or of the Queen of the Rosary? No doubt, the conversion of the heretics who surrounded him, but also—we are surely allowed to imagine—he asked and called with all his soul for the future legions of preachers; for the conquering work that would multiply him and perpetuate him in the Church; for those lights of the world, those athletes of faith, those preachers who would be the future workers for a harvest whose growing dawn he already perceived on the horizon. For them, without limit or respite, he offered prayers and weariness, tears and sacrifices—in a word, the best of his life.

Here, then, is where our religious calling still draws its life. After its awakening in God, in the home of eternal love, it springs up from the very depths of Dominic's soul. We are children of his heart, the fruits of his prayer, the recompense of his blood.

Consequently, during these days of the centenary, on seeing our blessed father so gloriously extolled, we should not be content with the thrill of a holy and filial pride, but rather be aware of the duty that is imposed. Before the Catholic world that admires and praises him, let sing and vibrate, even more ardently in the depths of our heart, the filial tenderness that we owe him. He is our father; it is from his gift that our Dominican life was born. Let us be his genuine children.

CHARACTERISTICS OF THE DEVOTION TO ST. DOMINIC

But how are we to put into action our devotion to St. Dominic? If, for that beloved father, the heart of his children ought to be ablaze, what would its flame be like? This we will try to express.

IN THE GIFT OF THE HOLY PATRIARCH

The splendor of a fireplace is measured by the range of its radiance; the glory of founders of orders, by the extent and the perfection of their survival. Their genuine triumph is to witness the eternal idea in which they were expressed perpetuate itself throughout the centuries; it is for them to live again in the souls of their children. It is to find oneself again in them, in the truth of their grace and of their spirit, in that same breath of life which uplifts the heart and makes it beat. This is the glory and the profound joy of the patriarchs of religious life. This is the glory and the joy of Dominic.

THE EXAMPLE OF OUR SAINTS

Consequently, this is the ambition incumbent on the Dominican soul. An ambition, that we like to say, was always dynamic and effective during the centuries of the Order's history. From this viewpoint, the biographies of our saints are greatly informative. It was by following in the tracks of St. Dominic, in a way, that they advanced in life. To get closer to him, to unite with him, to merge with him in ever-increasing perfection, that was their unceasing desire. If we were to get into details, it would be easy to prove, but this would take us too far astray. Allow me simply to cite a very recent example, which, among all others, must speak to our souls: it is borrowed from the life of Very Reverend Father Cormier, whom many of us knew and loved. In the heart of that venerated father, St. Dominic lived in an intensity of thought, of truly admirable love. To look upon him, to study him, to imitate him, to make him live again, these were his ever present needs. "Oh, Dominic," he would often say, "come and live within us." Called to be the successor of St. Dominic in the governance of the Order, and searching for a motto that would express both the secret of his interior life and the spirit of his charge, his thought fell on the great words of St. Paul chosen by his pontiff Pius X as motto for his pontificate: "To restore all things in Christ" But to modify it in the sense of his Dominican gift, he would say: "To restore all things in St. Dominic," *Instaurare omnia in Dominico,* which is to say, to frame everything around his memory, to animate everything with his spirit, to invigorate everything in his gift, to consume everything in his charity. A magnificent ideal, one that cannot help but attract souls, vowed to a similar calling.

But how to bring this about? Here, it seems to me, are the means to be taken.

TO LIVE WITHIN HIS MEMORY

1. First of all, we ought to live habitually with the memory of St. Dominic, You know the proverb: *Ubi amor, ibi oculus.* Looking follows instinctively the inclination of the heart, this is a fact of experience, for whose truth everyone can vouch. When a congenial feeling awakens in us, without delay we wish to know who is its object. The eye seeks him, the thought follows; one cannot separate himself from that object.

Well, this is the first characteristic of our devotion for St. Dominic. Is there any need to insist on this, after all we have just said? Blessed source of our religious vocation, living example of our holiness, should not St. Dominic brighten, in the light of a faithful and unremitting remembrance, the road on which we walk every day? In our Dominican life, is this not like a first principle that should simultaneously direct to it the whole as well as its parts? Do we think of this often enough? Is it a chimera to think that certain souls, Dominicans by habit and by profession, are insufficiently so in their hearts in their relationships with the blessed father? His thought is a stranger to their remembrance, his name is cold on their lips, their life is insufficiently impregnated with the fragrance of his own. A rare exception, no doubt; but once again, is it chimeric?

GUARDING FULLY HIS IDEAL OF LIFE

2. The Dominican soul should not at all seek its ideal outside of St. Dominic; rather, it should love, conserve, and safeguard this very ideal in its attractive and virginal integrity. The soul must be careful not to transform this ideal, or more exactly not to deform it, following personal conceptions. It must accept the ideal such as God has created it. It is inappropriate for a religious to

consider creating an ideal for himself. He is incarnated by God Himself in the soul of the founder. The latter's paternal soul expresses in dynamic traits what ought to be the soul of his children. To accommodate and to subject to individualistic ideas the duties of his calling would be a gravely reprehensible tendency. In vain would we seek to mask such pretensions with better excuses; we should beware of any innovation that deviates from traditional practices. On this point, to remain faithful to St. Dominic is in reality to remain faithful to the will of God Himself.

TO APPRECIATE THIS IDEAL MORE PROFOUNDLY

3. We should strive to penetrate and to lose ourselves in an ever deepening knowledge of the Dominican ideal that we have thus carefully preserved, and, on occasion, strongly defended.

When an artist wishes to paint a portrait, he places the person before him and is not content with a quick glance; he requires many and prolonged sittings. With greater reason, a long and patient study becomes imperative when it is a question of reproducing not only a flesh and blood face, but a soul, the soul of a saint, the soul of St. Dominic, wherein the human is almost blotted out and disappears in the splendor of the divine; this requires intensive study. What am I trying to say? The very study would be insufficient. Above and beyond human effort, the grace of God is required; prayer needs to be joined to study. It is especially true that in meditation and in prayer the mystery fades away and the brightness of grace, the genuine countenance of saints is revealed. Only the Spirit of God, who creates saints, can reveal them to us; he only will manifest the interior reality of St. Dominic. It is only in his light that the gentle and glorious appearance of our father will emerge from the shadows where it is hidden, to make itself known to our interior gaze, in the overpowering brightness of his sanctity and of his virtues.

To Find Again the Soul of our Father
and to Give it New Life

4. But true devotion cannot restrict itself to simple knowledge, however profound it be. After having sated itself with the sight of the beloved object, it seeks to unite itself to it, to assimilate it, to enter into as perfect as possible a union with it. This is the irresistible tendency of love. *Amicitia pares invenit aut facit.* [Friendship seeks equals or creates them.]

Indeed, this is what the soul, taken up by St. Dominic, wants to do and must accomplish. It seeks to make him live again, which is the great obligation of its calling: a glorious obligation but also how painstaking and unpleasant! We should not forget that St. Dominic lives on the highest peaks, the peaks of God; there, he pitches his interior and apostolic tent. In his life, God was not a mere remembrance, a brief pause, a passing event, but a habitual dwelling, a permanent relationship, an unceasing sharing in His entire being, an unending flow of all his being into His life was always a desirable look, a desire never fully satisfied, a movement that always uplifted. Moreover, in this vision, this desire, this movement, the soul, with all its sway, comes by, earnest, thirsty, finding there its rest and its happiness—a rest that simultaneously satisfies and increases appetite, delves into the soul and fills it.

But that is not all. Just as the life of God lies not entirely in the mystery of His intimate communications, but also in that it spreads outwardly in the irresistible bound of infinite goodness, so too the life of St. Dominic is not consumed in the divine fullness which is its share; it causes its superabundance to spring outwardly, to his apostolic life, his consuming zeal, the gains of his apostolate.

Yet, in the midst of his human activities, this is always a divine apostolate. However far his zeal carries him, following the example of God in his heart—Who gives Himself fully without ever taking leave of Himself—Dominic also gave himself over to souls without ever descending from the heights he inhabits, without ever leaving the companionship of God Who possesses him, always fixed on God, his center and his rest. The more he is held back by heaven, the more is he offered to the earth. Here you have St. Dominic!

A DIFFICULT BUT ATTAINABLE TASK

Yes, one must agree: the Dominican calling is a demanding one. Just as for the Kingdom of heaven, it is true to say that only the strong can seize it.

Nonetheless, I hasten to add, even if climbing the heights to which Dominic calls his children requires effort, climbing always remains possible. For the soul intent on perfection, the duty to climb and to soar is always accompanied by the necessary graces. God never refuses His help to the soul of good will.

How can this help be obtained?

BY OUR FILIAL TRUST

5. The answer is simple: by a totally filial trust in St. Dominic. As an ideal arising from our desires, it is, simultaneously, the paternal support for our weakness. The duty of coming to our aid is called for, in a way, by his heart. To be a father, is this not to give of oneself, and to give the best of what one has? Dominic is a father. The very loving father of all souls, without exception, who compose his religious family. By his calling as patriarch he is bound to help us.

6. Not only is he obliged to help us, he is able to do so. To that end, he has superabundant powers; his grace is not only personal, but also one of status, a basic grace, a fullness of grace, in which his family finds all the help necessary to attain the religious and Dominican goal. To his assembled children in tears around his bed of agony, the dying Dominic, fully conscious of that influence, said: "My children, do not weep. . . I will be more useful to you up there where I am going than I am here on

earth." Is it not timely and consoling to recall here this loving secret made to the religious of Citeaux, for whom he had a lively affection: "I assure you of one thing I never told anyone before and which I ask you to keep secret up to my death: that is, in this life, the Lord has never refused me anything I asked of him." "Father, if this is the case," said a monk, "why do you not ask master Conrad, whose fellowship the brothers strongly desire, to enter the Order?" "Dear Father," replied Dominic, "you speak there of a very difficult matter, but if you wish to spend the night in prayer with me, I am confident that the Savior will grant you this grace." After a night of prayer, at the first hour of the day, young Conrad came knocking on the door of the monastery, and, prostrating at the feet of St. Dominic, asked him for the habit of his Order.

7. Not only can Dominic help us, even more, he wants to help us. What is more touching in life than his paternal tenderness for his children? From the interior of Spain, he brings to his daughters at Prouille some wooden spoons. He

traveled on foot, never allowing his companions on the road to carry his baggage. At night, he interrupted his vigils and his prayers, he walked through the dormitories, visiting the brothers in their sleep. In the course of his journeys, he obtained a miracle to comfort a cooperator brother, worn out and faltering. On several occasions, he multiplied bread to supply the needs of the community. Not only did he work miracles for necessities but occasionally to give to his children the pleasing and the superfluous. Recall that in the parlor of San Sisto, where he had passed around among the brothers and sisters a miraculous cup from which each one drank freely, to satisfy thirst, without the contents ever being drained.

Not only does the deference of St. Dominic supply for the needs of his children, but it is very mercifully apparent even in their weaknesses. Thus, at Prouille, on the day of the dispersion of friars— sent throughout the world to preach, found convents, and this without resources or money— one of them, John of Navarre, refused to leave under such conditions. Moved to find a friar preacher with so little confidence in Providence, Dominic began to cry and fell to the feet of that child of little faith, but to no avail. He was unable to overcome his obstinacy; finally, in pity for such weakness, he had twelve coins presented to him— true mercy of a fatherly heart! Let us go to him, then, with fullest confidence.

BY A HABITUAL AND DEEP AFFECTION

Moreover, if we need to say more, let us not go to him only in our hours of distress; that would be too egotistical, unworthy even of our vocation. It is not on the needs of one day that we should base our confidence; it must be supported by a higher reality, totally independent of the created world and of the ephemeral. It must be based on God Himself, on that adorable will that, always animated, in time and place, subsequently invites us and directs us. In this is to be found the solid base of our devotion to St. Dominic.

Accordingly, it is not an optional devotion, by which we can choose to live or remain disinterested. By the very constraint of our destiny, it directs us.

It is not a momentary devotion, intermittent, a short-lived impression, a lightning bolt that shines then disappears, but a stable disposition, a habitual and permanent state, the necessary flow of a life whose source is, within us, always flowing and bubbling.

It is not a devotion of formulas and practices, a devotion of feeling, evolving on the edge of our spiritual life, but a reality, interior and deep, in a strong tie of union with God, the supreme goal of our vocation.

Therefore, it is in the very center of our spiritual life that devotion to St. Dominic finds its roots. It is one of its most precious riches, one of those most powerful and most active springboards.

BY AN ARDENT SHARING IN HIS LIFE

Consequently, as we have said, our devotion must not only keep the soul in the presence of St. Dominic, not only approach him from the heart with a very filial attraction, but especially with more efficacious and more decisive enthusiasm. Our devotion must uplift the soul, bring it to a state of union and of genuine intimacy with this beloved father—to that unity which is, par excellence, the very goal of love.

The perfection of the Christian soul consists in reliving Christ in His fulness, in such a manner as to be able to say with the Apostle, in all truth: "It is no longer I who live but it is Christ who lives in me." [*Gal* 2:20] The perfection of the Dominican soul could not be different, although it has a special modality, which is its knowledge and power. It relives Christ but in St. Dominic, in the particular gift of St. Dominic. It does not walk alone to its achievements; it walks with all the riches and all the powers of its beloved father, in dynamic and unceasing companionship with his virtues, dispositions, feelings, intentions, merits, love, mysteries—with all that he is, because, in truth, all of this is part of his gifts; it is his inheritance and his legacy. If "all that belongs to the Son belongs to the Father," all that is in the Father is in the Son. Fully convinced of the rights of supernatural sonship, this gift enters, by a lively faith, into the heart and the life of the blessed father; with an intense desire, it appropriates all that he is and all that he has. Like Jacob, in the garb of Esau, it reveals his personal insignificance, his poverty, and his inadequacy, but also the splendor of his gifts and of his merits. Thus garbed, transfigured, and in a way, imbued with the irresistible enthusiasm of a filial confidence, this perfection advances in its Dominican life toward the possession of its God and to its transformation in Christ.

Oh! If only we understood our attractive calling in this way. If we considered it in that permanent union with St. Dominic; if we were convinced that it is a vital and profound friendship, an unceasing fellowship with his life, an incessant interchange of love with his soul, a society, a fusion, a penetration, a unity as perfect as possible, a burst of enthusiasm and a springboard for all our efforts and for our every moment so as to realize all this without delay—how our life would be transformed! What holy growth! What energy, what effectiveness for the apostolate! What splendor for the Order! What help to the Church, what glory for God!

May our religious and Dominican life, therefore, be imbued ever more and more in this intimacy with our blessed father. On the road we are traveling, a road so filled with trials of all kinds, may Dominic always be with us and in us, as enlightenment for our ignorance, support for our weaknesses, consolation in our worries; a confidant in our joys, a companion in our battles, a model for our efforts, the faithful guardian of our interests, the support for our perseverance. Thus, will be fully achieved that spiritual paternity with which God has clothed him for our benefit. Thus also, will our vocation grow in the fulness of the gift. To the degree that we be more perfect Dominicans, we will also be all the more religious, all the more holy.

In his humility, the dying Dominic wished to be buried at the feet of his brothers. But you clearly understand that it is not under our feet that he ought to rest and abide, but in the deepest intimacy of our being. I do not hesitate to say that, this rest in the very hearts of his children will be more precious to him than the splendor of that precious mausoleum that holds his remains and that human ingenuity—in one of its unsullied inspirations—raised up for him in the church of the convent of Bologna. Accordingly, we will deserve to have realized for us the consoling promise of the Holy Spirit in Ecclesiasticus [*Sir* 3:8]: *In opere et sermone honora patrem tuum, ut superveniat tibi benedictio. (The blessing of patriarchs symbolizes the assurance that the blessing of the Most High will be our inheritance).* May this be the benefit of this centenary and the reward for the enthusiasm with which we will have celebrated it.

The brilliance of the centenary in Southern France, the cradle of the Order

The convents of the Province vied with each other to give this centenary a brightness worthy of their filial devotion. It is a lively joy for me to state this.

Toulouse gave the signal with an incomparable solemnity that was magnified by the presence and the words of the Very Reverend Master General of the Order. Marseille, Biarrtz, Bordeaux followed with greatly appreciated enthusiasm. Moreover, tomorrow, St. Maximin will close these manifestations with a piety no less dynamic and fitting because of the important place it occupies in the province. The monasteries of our sisters, after that of Prouille, also held their solemnities. Beyond the oceans, even our mission in Brazil echoed the festivities in France. From the *triduum* celebrated in Rio de Janeiro, presided over by His Excellency the Apostolic Nuncio, to the festivities celebrated at Conceiçao de Araguaya by Bishop Sebastian Thomas in his new cathedral—inaugurated and consecrated on that same day—St. Dominic was highly honored and praised. The province fittingly paid tribute to the glory of its blessed father.

This duty was particularly incumbent on the province's heart. It could not overlook the fact that this Southern part of France was the cradle chosen by God for the foundation of the Order of Friars Preachers. Under its skies, Dominic heard the divine call to the apostolate, and in its wake, he planted the first seeds of that magnificent tree which, for these many centuries, has covered the world with its mighty boughs.

With filial confidence in St. Dominic, may the province of Toulouse find in this gift of its origins a generous fidelity to the resolutions that must flow from this centenary celebration.

RESOLUTIONS FOR OUR LIFE

Yet, who will inform us of these resolutions? It is useless to search very far; let us ask St. Dominic himself to tell us. Let us interrogate his fatherly heart, at the final hour of his death, at a time when the soul, already released from the earth, alone in the presence of its God, contemplates the truth in a brilliant light and already speaks the words of eternal life: from his dying lips let us gather the highest revelation of our calling.

This death, the worthy coronation of a life all divine, adorns itself with a characteristic of striking nobility. Dominic had received a revelation of it. One day, when he ardently longed for the dissolution of his body, Our Lord, in the form of a very handsome young man, appeared to him. "Come, my beloved," he told him, "come to the home of eternal joy." A few days later, in Bologna, on returning from a tiring voyage, a violent fever seized him. To offer him some respite and to have him breathe a more refined air, he was taken to the countryside; but with the fever continuing unabated, he asked to return to the monastery. He wished to die in the midst of his children, to be buried under their feet. Around his death-bed, he first called the novices and with the most gentle words, exhorted them to discharge faithfully the duties of their vocation. Then he called for twelve of the oldest friars, and in their presence, out loud, made to

Brother Ventura the general confession of his own life. At its end, he added:

> Up to this day, the mercy of God has kept for me a pure flesh and a virginity without stain. Should you desire a similar blessing, avoid all suspicious relationships. It is the protection of this virtue that makes the servant agreeable to Christ, and that gives him glory and credit before the people.
>
> Persevere in serving the Lord in the fervor of the Spirit. Strive to spread the Order, which is only beginning.
>
> Remain grounded in sanctity and in regular observance.
>
> Keep growing in virtue.

THE FATHER'S TESTAMENT

This said, after having placed in high relief the purity of the friar preacher, his love for the Order, the enthusiasm that must animate him, his application to the holy observances, the commitment to genuine holiness, Dominic's voice took on a more solemn tone, as if, in this

49

development of Dominican life, he wanted to go further and climb even higher. Using the sacred form of the testament, he added: "My beloved brothers, here is the heritage I leave you, as my genuine children: have charity, preserve humility, embrace voluntary poverty."

With these words and with his earthly mission completed, as Dominic faced eternity he made this prayer: 'Holy Father, I have accomplished your will; those whom You have given me, I have preserved. Now, I commend them to You; keep them, watch over them.'

These were his last words. In the supreme effort that expressed to his sons his wishes as patriarch and father, his heart stopped beating.

Here you have the testament of Dominic. Let us keep this testament in filial piety; let it be the genuine treasure of religious souls, the shining beacon of our life.

A testament is always a sacred matter, all the more reason when it is the testament of a father, if the father is a saint, and a glorious saint among all others. How imposing, then, his authority! What veneration is awakened in the heart of his children!

The testament of St. Dominic is admirable; in its substantial brevity, the spiritual life is fully concentrated and dynamic.

"Have charity," that is to say, live with the life of God Himself, since God is charity. "He who remains in charity remains in God and God lives within him." [See *I Jn* 4:16] In these simple and brief words, the life of the friar preacher is fully directed and fixed, and even admirably raised to the heights where it is destined to flourish and to shine.

But, here below, man carries this treasure of charity and of divine life in a fragile vase, the vase of his fallen nature. Dominic does not ignore this, which is why he adds: "Embrace voluntary poverty," thereby pushing away the enemy *outside*: cupidity, [the love of money] "the source of all evils." [*I Tim* 6:10] Moreover, he adds: "Preserve humility," a direct and decisive blow against the enemy *within*: the ego, self-love, home of all covetousness and of all revolt.

51

There you have it, the final instructions in the struggles for holiness and for the apostolate— a dynamic affirmation of what he himself had always been. Poor, with a poverty that reduced him to the strictly necessary; humble, with a humility that in everything kept him beneath the feet of every creature; and in a radiant purity, consequence of those self-denials, living in admirable fulness the life of charity, the very life of God.

This life of God, this life in God, is basically what characterizes Dominic. Did not his contemporaries tell us that he spoke always and only about God or with God? *De Deo vel cum Deo.* These words, that so portray his soul and seem to be the genuine bywords of his life, he desired to have engraved in the Book of Constitutions of his Order.

Today, in them, he continues to shine, setting perpetually, with an indelible trait, the description of the friar preacher.

Let us especially engrave these sacred words—the beacon star of our Dominican vocation—in the most intimate depths of our hearts. Thus, following the example of St. Dominic and the lofty words of St. Paul, we will be "men of God."

IN OUR EXILE, OUR PRAYER TO OUR FATHER

The dispositions that at the hour of his death and with such strong insistence the holy patriarch enjoined on his children, witnesses to his demise, he demands again and always from our very selves. Going beyond time and space, his vision crosses the centuries, his word reaches his entire posterity and addresses each one of us. Let us acknowledge the voice of our father, and finally give answer to his appeal, as we labor to become, like him, men of God. In these few words are distilled all sanctity and all greatness. May our best efforts be focused on bringing them about in our Dominican life. From now on, may they be the sole object of our desires, in the beautiful prayer to St. Dominic, familiar to our lips and with which I fondly close:

O wonderful hope which, at the hour of your death, you left to your grieving brothers, promising your paternal help in their distress. Fulfill, Father, what you have promised; help us by your prayers. You who by so many miracles have manifested your influence, bring us heaven's help; put an end to the evils that have befallen us. Fulfill, Father, what you have promised; help us by your prayers. For the glory of the Father, the glory of the Son, and the glory of the Holy Spirit. Fulfill, Father, what you have promised; help us by your prayers.

May St. Dominic hear this appeal from our souls and bless our province of Toulouse.

The Holy Day of Easter, 21 April 1935,
Marseille, Convent of St. Lazarus.

Friar J.-Marie Étienne VAYSSIÈRE, OP
Provincial of Toulouse

www.ingramcontent.com/pod-product-compliance
Lightning Source LLC
Chambersburg PA
CBHW060538030426
42337CB00021B/4322